GRAPHIC LIBRARY®

INVENTIONS AND DISCOVERY

LOUIS PASTEUR and PASTEURIZATION

Jennifer Fandel

illustrated by Keith Wilson,
Rodney Ramos,
and Charles Barnett

Raintree

www.raintreepublishers.co.uk
Visit our website to find out
more information about
Raintree books.

Phone 0845 6044371
Fax +44 (0) 1865 312263
Email myorders@capstonepub.co.uk

Customers from outside the UK please telephone +44 1865 312262

Raintree is an imprint of Capstone Global Library Limited, a company incorporated in England
and Wales having its registered office at 7 Pilgrim Street, London, EC4V 6LB – Registered
company number: 6695582

"Raintree" is a registered trademark of Pearson Education Limited, under licence to Capstone
Global Library Limited

Design: Alison Thiele
Colourist: Tami Collins
UK editor: Diyan Leake
Originated by Capstone Global Library Ltd
Printed in China by South China Printing Company Ltd

ISBN 978 1 406 21570 0 (hardback)
14 13 12 11 10
10 9 8 7 6 5 4 3 2 1

British Library Cataloguing in Publication Data
Fandel, Jennifer -- Louis Pasteur and pasteurization
A full catalogue record for this book is available from the British Library.

Editor's note: Direct quotations from primary sources are indicated by a yellow background.

Direct quotations appear on the following pages:

Page 10, from the Oxford Dictionary of Quotations (New York: Oxford University Press, 1999).
Page 11, quoted in *Louis Pasteur* by Patrice Debre (Baltimore: Johns Hopkins University
Press, 1998).

CONTENTS

CHAPTER 1
HAZARDOUS FOOD

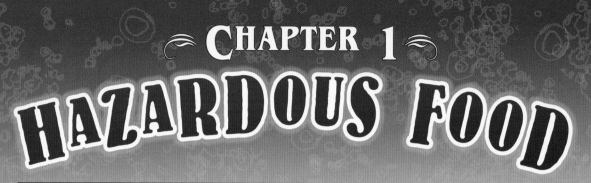

In the mid-1800s, people didn't know that germs cause disease. They knew that micro-organisms existed, but they were believed to be harmless. Because no one knew that germs cause disease, no one knew how diseases spread.

Pierre has the beginning stages of a disease called tuberculosis, but he wouldn't think to wash his hand after coughing into it.

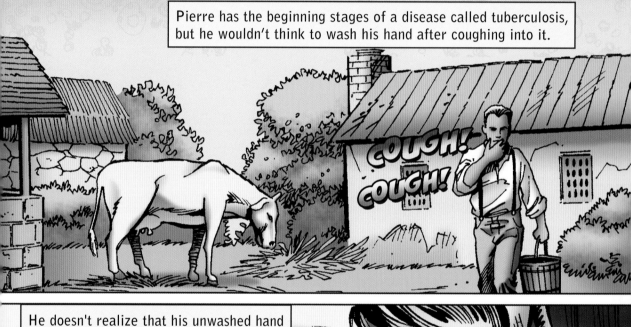

COUGH!
COUGH!

He doesn't realize that his unwashed hand sent thousands of tiny germs into the milk he gathered from the family cow.

Countless people died from disease carried in unsafe food.

But things were changing. In the mid-1800s, French chemist Louis Pasteur began to research food spoilage. Slowly, the mysterious connection between food and disease-causing germs would be uncovered.

7

CHAPTER 2
A LIVING PROCESS

In 1854, Pasteur was the head of a college in Lille, France. His job led him to resolve problems occurring in the community. In 1856, he visited Mr Bigo, a beet alcohol producer with a spoilage problem.

My beet alcohol is ruined. The beets are fine, but the alcohol keeps spoiling.

May I take some samples of the alcohol? Both good and bad batches?

Of course.

Back at his lab, Pasteur looked at the samples under a microscope.

Interesting.

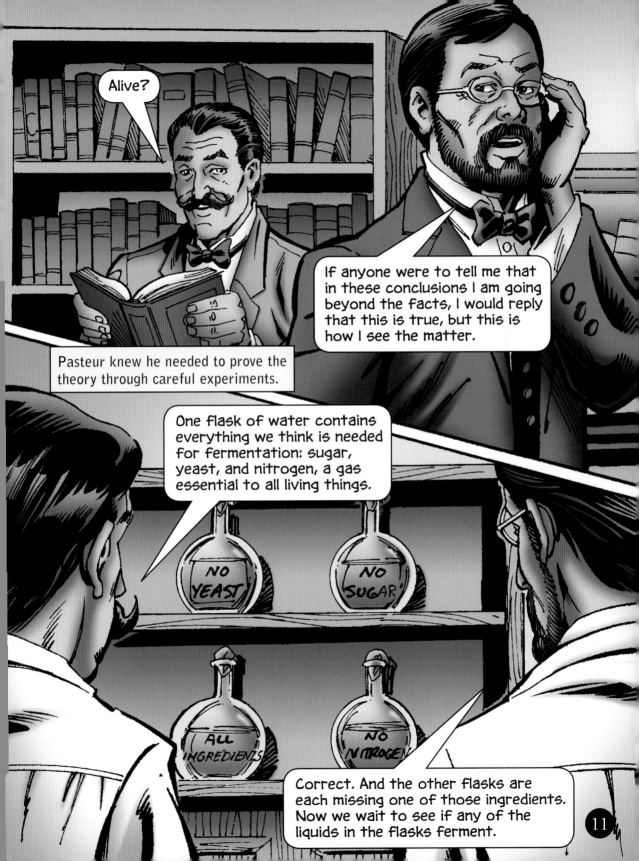

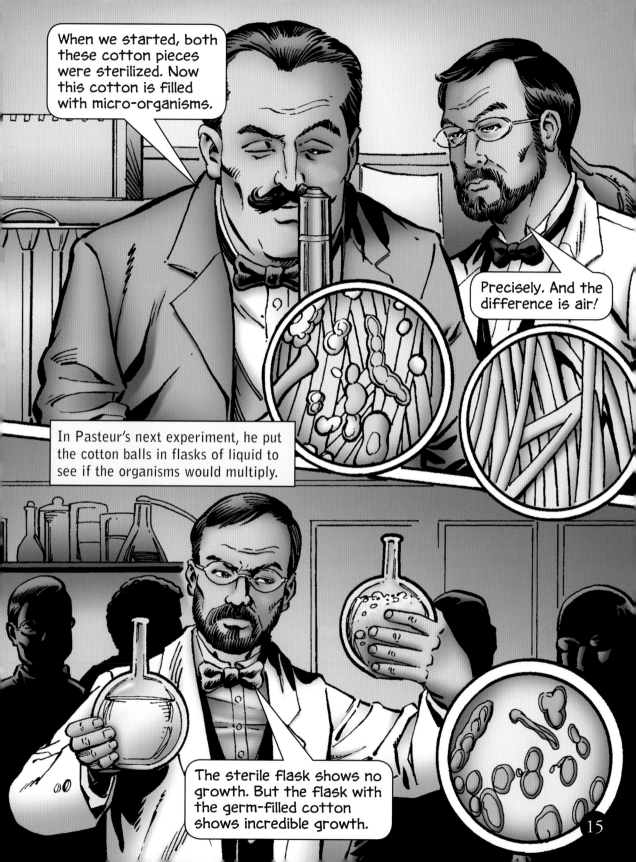

Pasteur wondered if micro-organisms always grew so easily. In his studies during 1860, he opened sealed flasks of liquid in different places to see if different conditions, such as temperature, affected the growth of micro-organisms.

Warm, moist conditions seem to encourage growth.

Hot, dry conditions keep growth down.

And cold nearly stops growth.

From these studies, Pasteur hoped to disprove the theory of spontaneous generation. Many scientists believed that micro-organisms came from a mysterious "life force" in the air.

The swan-necked shape should trap germs in the bends but still allow air into the flask.

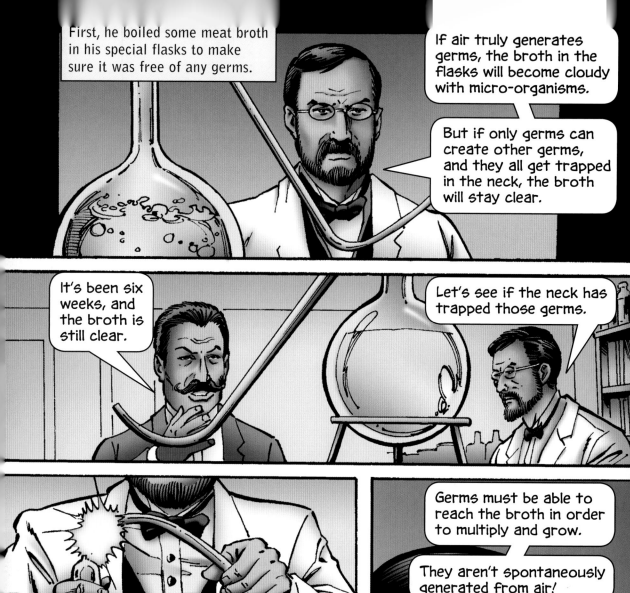

First, he boiled some meat broth in his special flasks to make sure it was free of any germs.

If air truly generates germs, the broth in the flasks will become cloudy with micro-organisms.

But if only germs can create other germs, and they all get trapped in the neck, the broth will stay clear.

It's been six weeks, and the broth is still clear.

Let's see if the neck has trapped those germs.

Once the swan neck was placed in the solution, germs grew in only 36 hours.

Germs must be able to reach the broth in order to multiply and grow.

They aren't spontaneously generated from air!

17

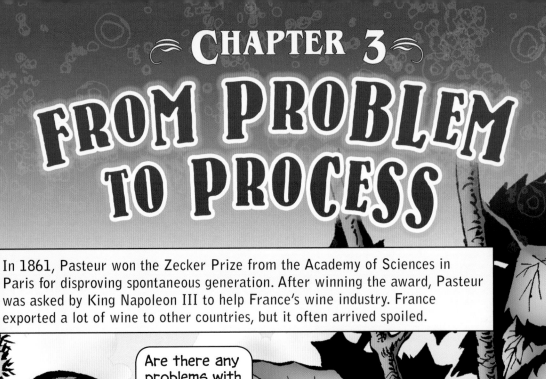

CHAPTER 3

FROM PROBLEM TO PROCESS

In 1861, Pasteur won the Zecker Prize from the Academy of Sciences in Paris for disproving spontaneous generation. After winning the award, Pasteur was asked by King Napoleon III to help France's wine industry. France exported a lot of wine to other countries, but it often arrived spoiled.

19

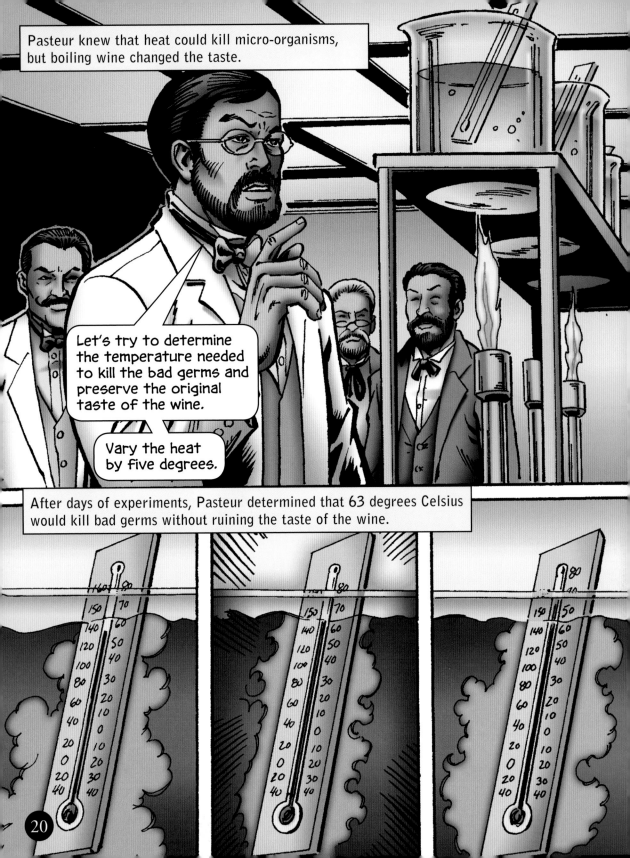

Pasteur knew that heat could kill micro-organisms, but boiling wine changed the taste.

Let's try to determine the temperature needed to kill the bad germs and preserve the original taste of the wine.

Vary the heat by five degrees.

After days of experiments, Pasteur determined that 63 degrees Celsius would kill bad germs without ruining the taste of the wine.

Pasteur also determined the wine should be heated for 30 minutes to prevent spoiling.

Cold slows growth, so the heat-treated wine should be moved to a cold tank to keep it from developing new germs. We'll bring in cold spring water to cool it.

Pasteur and his assistants tested the entire process and then checked on the wine.

No harmful micro-organisms are present! The process worked!

And it tastes great.

Pasteur took out a patent in 1865, calling the process pasteurization.

21

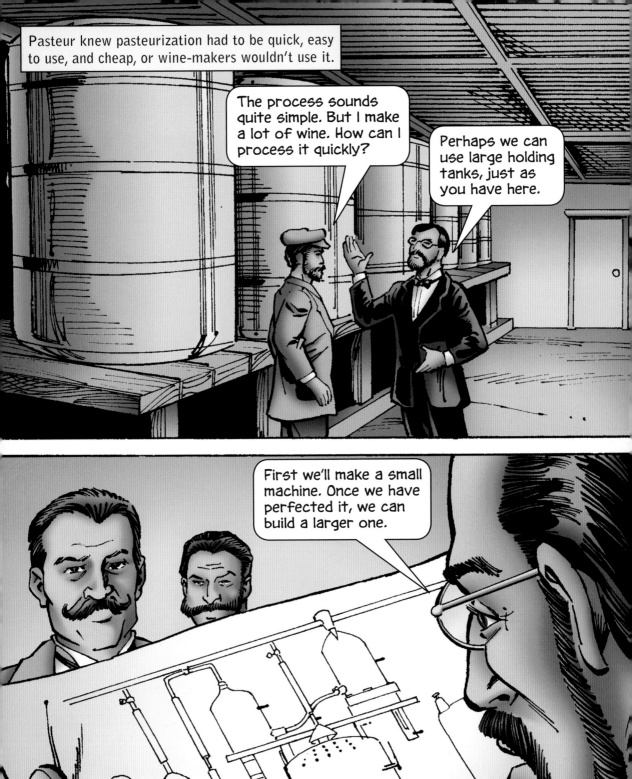

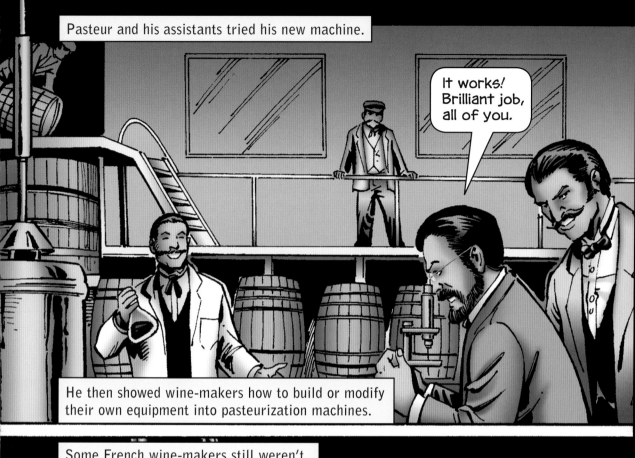

Pasteur and his assistants tried his new machine.

It works! Brilliant job, all of you.

He then showed wine-makers how to build or modify their own equipment into pasteurization machines.

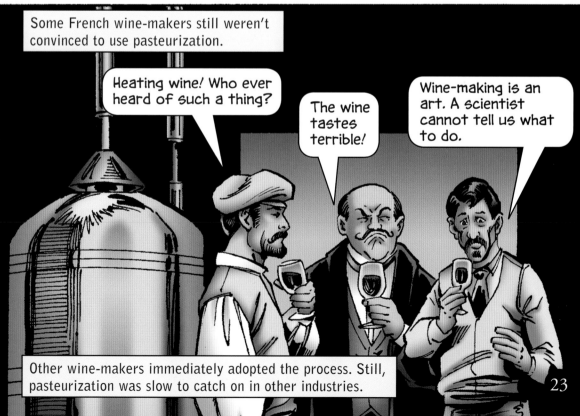

Some French wine-makers still weren't convinced to use pasteurization.

Heating wine! Who ever heard of such a thing?

The wine tastes terrible!

Wine-making is an art. A scientist cannot tell us what to do.

Other wine-makers immediately adopted the process. Still, pasteurization was slow to catch on in other industries.

23

CHAPTER 4
PASTEURIZATION FOR HEALTH

Louis Pasteur's work with germs made him an early supporter of the germ theory of disease. Soon, new discoveries about germs would give pasteurization a new purpose.

In 1882, Robert Koch made a startling announcement.

I have identified the tuberculosis bacteria and proven that it causes the disease.

Today, pasteurization continues to make milk safe to drink. Thanks to the work of Louis Pasteur in the 1800s, people became more aware of the science behind our food supply.

27

MORE ABOUT

LOUIS PASTEUR
~ and ~

PASTEURIZATION

 Louis Pasteur was born in 1822 in France. He died in 1895. At the time of his death, he was considered a hero in France. The government ordered a state funeral, an honour usually given to a country's president or king. Many citizens joined the funeral procession in the streets of Paris.

 Pasteur and his wife Marie had five children, but only two lived past childhood. Two died of typhoid, a disease that attacks the intestines, while an unknown disease struck the other child. The deaths of his children motivated Pasteur to study diseases and learn to prevent them.

 Pasteur was very protective of his work. Even on holiday, Pasteur took his notebooks that contained the details of his experiments with him. He kept extremely detailed notes, numbering around 10,000 pages.

 Pasteurization helps kill bacteria that can show up in milk supplies. Some of the deadly diseases it can prevent are typhoid fever, tuberculosis, scarlet fever, and polio.

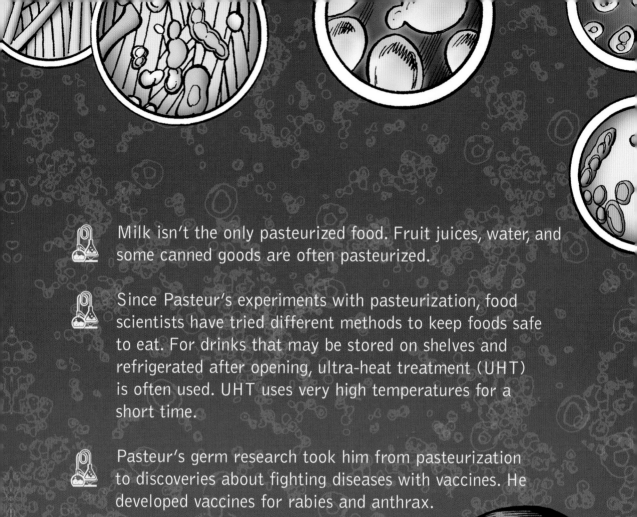

Milk isn't the only pasteurized food. Fruit juices, water, and some canned goods are often pasteurized.

Since Pasteur's experiments with pasteurization, food scientists have tried different methods to keep foods safe to eat. For drinks that may be stored on shelves and refrigerated after opening, ultra-heat treatment (UHT) is often used. UHT uses very high temperatures for a short time.

Pasteur's germ research took him from pasteurization to discoveries about fighting diseases with vaccines. He developed vaccines for rabies and anthrax.

GLOSSARY

bacteria microscopic living things. Some bacteria cause disease.

germ micro-organism. The word *germs* is usually used for micro-organisms that make people ill.

micro-organism living thing too small to be seen without a microscope

patent legal document that gives an inventor the right to make, use, or sell an invention for a set number of years

tuberculosis a disease caused by bacteria that causes fever, weight loss, and coughing. Left untreated, tuberculosis can lead to death.

yeast a kind of micro-organism called a fungus that causes dough to rise and alcohol to form

INTERNET SITES

http://www.invent.org
Click on the "Hall of Fame" tab and enter "Pasteur" in the Search field for a profile of the life and work of Louis Pasteur.

http://www.bbc.co.uk/history/historic_figures/pasteur_louis.shtml
This web page provides a biography of Louis Pasteur.

MORE BOOKS TO READ

The Fight Against Microbes: Pasteur's Story,
C. Birmingham (Mathew Price Ltd, 2006)

Inventions and Investigations, Andrew Solway (Raintree, 2010)

Louis Pasteur (Levelled Biographies: Great Scientists series),
Liz Miles (Heinemann Library, 2009)

Scalpels, Stitches and Scars (A Painful History of Medicine
series), John Townsend (Raintree, 2007)

World's Worst Germs: Micro-organisms and Disease, Anna
Claybourne (Raintree, 2006)

FIND OUT MORE

The Pasteur Institute has a museum devoted to Louis Pasteur
where you can visit his laboratory, follow the progress of his
research, walk through his living quarters, and see his tomb.
Pasteur Institute
25 rue du Dr-Roux F
75015 Paris
Telephone: +33 (0)1 45 68 82 83
http://www.pasteur.fr/ip/easysite/go/03b-000029-049/institut-
pasteur

Visit a dairy in your area where you can see how pasteurization
in done.

INDEX